Careers in Architecture

your questions and answers

Thomas Lee

TROTMAN

This first edition published in 1997 in Great Britain by Trotman and Company Limited, 12 Hill Rise, Richmond, Surrey TW10 6UA

© Trotman and Company Limited 1997

British Library Cataloguing in Publication Data

A catalogue record for this book is available from the British Library

ISBN 0 85660 282 5

Printed and bound in Great Britain by Redwood Books

Contents

What about working in architecture?

'An art for all to learn because all are concerned with it.'
John Ruskin

Look around you: the chances are that you are currently situated in or near some form of building. The fact is that no matter where you live or what you do, every human being has a primary requirement for shelter, security and privacy. Architecture is therefore of fundamental importance to us all.

In primitive society the person seeking these requirements was also responsible for providing them – whether by using a natural feature such as a cave, or by using the materials available to construct a basic dwelling such as a mud hut or wigwam. Client, architect and builder were therefore one and the same person.

As society became more complex, there arose the need for more permanent structures. In addition to the basic dwelling there began to emerge the demand for places and structures to accommodate social functions such as worship, entertainment and general meeting and trading places, as well as accommodation for governments and great leaders. It is in these societies – such as Ancient Egypt – that we first see distinct building professions emerge. Skilled craftsmen would have been chosen for the construction of these large civic buildings, and the profession of architect was born.

Today there are literally hundreds of different professions and career opportunities available within the construction industry. These are broadly divisible into three groups: designers, builders and 'others'.

1

Designers

Among the design professions are architecture, engineering, interior design, landscape architecture and planning. Each design profession is supported by technicians and administrative staff.

Builders

The building profession consists on the one hand of a wide range of management jobs, and on the other of a large number of skilled building trades. It takes over 20 different skilled trades to construct a simple house.

Others

Together, building and design are supported, where necessary, by an almost infinite number of related specialist professions and businesses. Among them are acoustics specialists, architectural journalists, building materials manufacturers, computer-aided design (CAD) specialists, construction lawyers, land surveyors, lecturers, machinery designers and manufacturers, project management companies, photographers and quantity surveyors.

The role of the architect

The role of the architect is threefold: businessman (liaising with the client), designer (visualising the building in three dimensions and carrying out the detailed design) and manager (co-ordinating the other professionals involved with the project, known collectively as the 'design team'). Architects therefore occupy a central position within the industry as a whole.

An architect's work involves the initial conceptual design of the building, communication of this design to clients, the design team, builders and others, preparation of detailed design drawings for use on site, and the management of the building project from inception through to completion. The nature of the job means that there is

2

tremendous variety in an architect's work – both from project to project, and from day to day within the same project. No two building projects are the same. Each one will present new challenges in terms of balancing the client's requirements and budget with the design concept, embracing site and location characteristics, choice of materials, the requirements of the various regulatory authorities, accommodating the needs of the other design team members – the list is endless! Even if two buildings appear to be identical there will be aspects of each job which will be different: no two sites are ever the same, the requirements of the local planning authorities will vary, different people will be involved for each project, etc. In addition, the steel manufacturer who was used last time might be too far away for this site, or the bricks that were specified previously might no longer be available.

If you are creative, good at both arts and sciences, and interested in the built environment, then architecture could well be the career for you. Seeing your thoughts and ideas being converted into buildings which people will use and enjoy for years to come brings a real sense of achievement and satisfaction.

How do people work in architecture?

Architecture is one of a group of professional disciplines which makes up the construction industry. The industry provides not only all our buildings such as hospitals, cinemas, concert halls, sports stadiums, offices and houses – but also our airports, bridges, dams, water towers, power stations, railways and roads. Architects would not necessarily be involved in all of the above types of construction. For new projects where the primary concern is the structure's capacity to take loads (eg dams, bridges, roads), the chief designer and project coordinator would normally be a civil engineer. However, where the brief is to create a building which will be used at least in part to accommodate people, the central role would be that of an architect.

Architectural projects can last for anything from a few months for a small domestic conversion or extension up to 10–15 years or even longer for a large housing scheme or civic building such as a hospital or concert hall. Large projects can often involve hundreds of design professionals including a team of architects, each one handling a different aspect of the overall design. On smaller projects, however, the architect might be required also to play the part of interior designer, landscape architect, quantity surveyor and structural engineer!

Not all the work an architect does need necessarily be for 'live' projects (ie those which are definitely going to be built). Architects are often asked to prepare feasibility studies in which case a report, usually accompanied by drawings and photographs, will be prepared and presented, after which the client might decide not to go ahead. Much time can also be spent by aspiring young architectural practices preparing drawings for architectural competitions, simply to gain the prestige of winning.

In addition to the basic office-based design work, much of an architect's time will also be spent out of the office. Once a job is 'on site' (ie being built), regular site meetings will be held where the builder can discuss progress and other issues relating directly to the actual construction of the building with the architect, structural engineer and client. Land and building surveying are also skills which architects are required to have – and are of use especially on smaller projects where the architect might be used to measure a plot of land or an existing building rather than a separate firm of surveyors. Meetings with clients and other professionals will also frequently be held at locations other than the architects' office. For example, regular visits to fire service headquarters to discuss fire regulations with qualified personnel are an essential part of most building projects.

Planning applications

Nearly all architectural projects in the UK will require planning permission from the local authority within whose boundaries the site lies. This applies to building alterations, extensions, road alterations and changes of use for existing properties as well as to new buildings. Planning applications are prepared by the architect and include drawings, site photographs and models to show the site as it is, and the new building(s) as they will look. These are submitted to the local authority together with the appropriate forms and fee, for presentation to, and approval by, the council.

As part of this procedure, the architect's drawings must be made available for public inspection. If there are any objections raised to the proposals – perhaps by a member of the public – the architect might be asked to argue a case for the scheme during a council meeting.

When planning permission is granted it lasts for five years, and building work to the approved design may begin on that site at any time during this period.

Building Regulations

The second official set of drawings which has to be prepared by the architect is for Building Regulations approval. The Building Regulations are a set of documents published by the government and are designed to ensure that all construction work within the UK is carried out to certain standards. Different sections cover specific issues such as structure, heating, insulation, drainage and access for the disabled.

The architect prepares a set of detailed drawings showing exactly how the building is to be constructed. There is also a requirement to submit fairly detailed structural calculations at this stage. For most projects, these would normally be prepared by the civil engineer, although for small domestic projects the architect would prepare these calculations. Once the necessary drawings and documents are ready, the application is sent to the local authority which then responds either with approval or, more frequently, with a list of specific points which need to be addressed by the architect. Building Regulations approval is therefore a much more interactive process than that for planning permission, often involving numerous meetings and correspondence between architect and Building Control officer in order to get the building passed.

A copy of the current edition of the Building Regulations will be available in any good library.

What sorts of jobs are there?

In addition to architects and their immediate support staff, there is an almost infinite number of specialist careers within the wider architectural profession, making it accessible to people with a broad range of qualifications, talents and abilities. Among these are architectural historians, architectural journalists, construction lawyers, interior designers, landscape architects, lecturers, lighting or acoustics engineers, model-makers, perspective artists and photographers.

However, the number of different careers actually represented within the architects' office is quite small: typically including only architects, technicians and support staff (secretaries, accountants, etc).

Architect

The term 'architect' is a generic term like 'doctor' or 'lawyer' and is used to describe any qualified member of the profession. Only members of the Architects' Registration Council of the United Kingdom (ARCUK) are allowed by law to call themselves an architect. The role of an architect will vary considerably between practices, and according to his/her position within a particular practice. The architect at the head of a practice is usually more of a businessman than a designer, whose primary concerns would be attracting new clients and managing the company. A newly recruited architect might spend his or her first year working on certain detailed aspects of a number of existing projects before progressing on to running his or her own jobs.

Project architect

Most architects will soon reach the stage where they are running their own projects within a practice. The architect who is responsible for the conceptual design, detailed design and project management for a particular building is referred to as the project or job architect.

Once he or she has been assigned to a particular job, the first thing the project architect will have to do is develop a conceptual design which meets the requirements of the client, the characteristics of the site, and which satisfies the local planning authority and any other relevant regulatory bodies (eg English Heritage). This conceptual design, or scheme, is presented to the client and to other members of the design team using drawings, sketches, models and increasingly, computer techniques. Once the scheme has been approved by the client, and planning permission has been gained, the project architect will begin work on the detailed design of the building.

For most building projects, the detailed design is the most time-consuming element of the project architect's work. This involves developing the building design in consultation with other professionals such as the structural engineer and the fire officer, to a stage where a final set of detailed scale drawings can be produced for use on site by the builder. These drawings will also be presented to the quantity surveyor for use in producing the bill of quantities, and to the local authority for Building Regulations approval.

Among the detailed design drawings that the project architect is responsible for producing for a typical building project are:

Floor plans – a different drawing is produced for each floor of the building to show elements such as columns, walls, doors, windows, staircases, lifts, etc. These drawings will then be used as templates for producing a complete set of floor plans. Thus, new drawings of the same floor will be produced showing, for example, the heating system, the electrical system, the foundations, etc.

Site plan – this drawing is often based on the Ordnance Survey map of the site, or on a separate site survey carried out by the architect or an independent firm of land surveyors. The site plan shows how the new building will be positioned on the land and how it relates to other buildings or features of the site. Information typically found on a site plan would be details of the site boundaries (buildings, fences, rivers, roads, etc), a schematic map of the drainage system, any new site access or car parking provision, and details of all materials to be used externally such as road and pavement surfaces, walls or railings, and any 'soft' landscaping to be included such as grass, shrubs and trees.

Elevations – elevations are produced to show what the buildings look like from the sides. These are usually labelled using the points of the compass (the north elevation being the view looking from the north, not towards the north). Elevations will often include a drawing of existing adjacent buildings as well as the new building, and sometimes even trees, cars and people will be drawn in to show what the new development will look like to passers-by.

Sections – sections are drawings of what you would see if you were to slice through the building along an imaginary vertical line. Sections are frequently regarded as the most important design drawings as they are often the most revealing – even to the architect himself! Imagine a section through a typical house: you would see the foundations and ground floor construction, the way in which the walls were built including cavity, wall ties and insulation, lintels above windows and doors, the way in which the ceiling, floor joists and floor above are assembled, the attic, rafters and roof construction – none of which would normally be visible.

Projections – plans, sections and elevations are vital for the builder, but it is often difficult for the lay person to interpret such drawings and to gain an impression of how the project will actually look on the site in three dimensions. One of the simplest ways of giving a three-dimensional impression is to produce drawings known as 'isometric' or 'axonometric' projections. These are scale drawings created by projecting lines up from a plan, and although the image presented is slightly false owing to the lack of true perspective, projections are widely used by architects as a quick way of showing clients and others how the scheme will look.

The project architect will constantly refer to various technical manuals and draw extensively on the expertise of architectural technicians during the production of these drawings.

Architectural technologist (technician)

Architects employ architectural technologists (or technicians) to assist them with the detailed design and production of working drawings, and often rely on them to give advice and information about construction principles, specification of materials, etc. Technicians will frequently know considerably more about the 'nuts and bolts' of how a building is put together than the architect does, and it is not uncommon for an architect to pass over the majority of the detailed design to a technician or team of technicians.

Computer-aided design (CAD) technician

As with just about every other industry, the construction industry – and architecture in particular – has been dramatically affected by the increased widespread use of computers. During the past ten years, specialised computer programs for the production of working drawings and three-dimensional images have revolutionised the way in which architects work. Indeed, for many practices the use of computer-aided design (CAD) programs has become so important that many now employ specialist CAD technicians to do this work. The accuracy of the drawings produced, and ease of repetition of standard elements such as doors and windows, make this technique highly desirable for the production of drawings for use on site. Some of the more sophisticated programs are able to simulate 3D video productions of a 'walk' around and through the building, showing detail such as materials, colour schemes and the effects of natural and artificial lighting, before any building work has begun.

Secretarial support staff

As with all professional practices, the work undertaken by architects requires the backup of efficient secretarial staff – indeed perhaps more so because in addition to the normal letters and textual documents, architects' secretaries have to handle, file and print drawings (often A1 or A0 size), as well as deal with photographs, models, microfiche and computer images. It is crucial for any member of the secretarial team in an architects' office not only to have a good working knowledge of what an architect does, but also to be familiar with the day-to-day working methods and terminology used by all the other professionals in the field.

Interior designers

Most architectural projects will require the architect to think about both the external and internal appearances of the new building. However, there will be some projects where, for a variety of possible reasons, the client or architect chooses to appoint a specialist interior designer. Such projects might include an art gallery, concert hall or private house where the client will also be the owner of the building. The interior designer might become involved at an early stage to consult with the architect on matters such as natural lighting, choice of materials and colour schemes. Alternatively, the interior designer may be brought in to look at specialist issues such as furniture, fixtures and fittings after the building has been completed and the architect's work is done.

Landscape architect

One of the primary concerns for any architectural project is to strike a balance between the building that is being created and its natural environment. For buildings in inner city locations, the addition of trees and other plants both inside and around the site can have a dramatic effect on the new development. And for country locations where the new development might occupy a greenfield site, the handling of the natural environment is clearly of paramount importance. It is for this reason that landscape architects are being increasingly used by architects to handle this aspect of their work.

It is the job of the landscape architect to produce the landscape scheme for a building project, presented using drawings and models. Landscape architects are trained in the design of both 'hard' landscaping and

11

'soft' landscaping. Hard landscaping refers to any non-living building element used around the building, such as paving, brick walls, fencing and seating. Soft landscaping refers to all horticultural elements such as grass and trees. Landscape architects are very knowledgeable about the use, durability and weathering properties of different building materials, and the way they interact both physically and chemically with different plant species. They are not purely horticulturists.

Model-maker

One of the problems with two-dimensional line drawings as a means of communicating a three-dimensional design is that the client often finds it difficult to visualise the building and how it will look on its site. It is not uncommon for architects to make rough models as part of the normal design process, either for presentation to the client or simply to help their own understanding of the scheme they are designing. However, on larger projects, or where the budget permits, specialist architectural model-makers may be used. Model-makers produce scale models from the architect's drawings, which can range from simple block models to highly intricate scale replicas of the real building, incorporating appropriate materials, lighting, colour scheme and landscaping. For such projects it is not uncommon for the final model to account for around one per cent of the total cost of the project (models costing a million pounds or more are not unheard of).

Perspective artist

Another effective option for the architect working on a project where a model-maker would be too expensive, is to employ a perspective artist or illustrator. Often trained architects themselves, perspective artists produce full-colour paintings or drawings of the proposed building as it would look after it was built – complete with cars, people, landscaping and surrounding buildings. Another advantage of the perspective artist over the model-maker is the speed at which the work is done – in some cases a perspective artist briefed in the morning can have a fully rendered drawing ready by the end of the day.

Where will I work? Large or small employers?

The following table shows the proportion of all UK architects employed in practices of different sizes:

1–2 staff	30%
3–5 staff	18%
6–10 staff	15%
11–30 staff	22%
31–50 staff	7%
51+ staff	8%

It can be seen from these statistics that most architects currently employed in the UK work in companies with 30 or fewer employees, and nearly half in practices with fewer than 6 staff. One question often asked of architects is 'What is your area of specialisation?' The fact is, however, that most architects' practices do not operate within a particular specialist area. Architectural training equips the student with the skills to take on just about any project. Thus the factor governing the type of work undertaken by a particular practice is the size, or contract value, of the project. The higher the contract value, the fewer projects there will be, and the fewer practices there will be with sufficient staffing and resources to undertake the work.

Private practice

The vast majority of architects working in the UK are employed in private practice. Private practices range in size from the one-man band running a handful of small local projects, to the large international firm with several offices spread over more than one country and with hundreds of employees.

Design and build companies

Recent years have seen the establishment of an increasing number of companies which provide a complete building service – either to external clients or for their own use as developers. These 'Design and build' companies might employ in-house architects, or alternatively use architects from the private sector to carry out the design work.

Multidisciplinary companies

There are also a number of firms in which architects, engineers, surveyors and other building professionals work together for the same company. These multidisciplinary companies are generally larger than architects' firms, and have several advantages: they facilitate cross-fertilisation between the different disciplines eg clients looking for a surveyor can also be offered an architectural service; they avoid doubling up on secretarial and other support staff/services; and they avoid the need to approach outside companies when putting together the design team for each job. However, such companies are fairly inflexible, carry large overheads and can be more vulnerable during a recession.

Public sector

A survey carried out by RIBA in 1994 showed that 15% of UK architects worked for local authorities, and 9% worked in central government. However, the number of architects working in the public sector has decreased steadily during recent years. Many central government divisions have now been privatised, such as the Property

14

Services Agency. In addition, local authority architects' departments, although not privatised, are now required to compete with private architects for much of the work which previously would have been given to the department automatically. Although this has led to a more competitive arena where borough and county architects' offices are able to compete for work both in their immediate area and beyond, the net effect has been a decline in the amount of work undertaken by local authority architects' departments

However, although work within the public sector continues to slow down as privatisation continues, there are still jobs within this area. The main strength of public sector work is that, unlike many private practices, public sector architects do have a specific area of expertise, which makes them very competitive in their niche. The down side of this is that the work is often regarded as less exciting than private practice.

The work undertaken by a local authority architects' department would be primarily council-owned buildings such as courthouses, doctors' surgeries, leisure facilities, old peoples' homes, police buildings, schools and village halls. A typical office might contain between five and 10 architects and anywhere between five and 15 technicians, but again, this is decreasing.

The architects' office

Architects' offices are almost invariably open plan as this facilitates the dialogue and 'bouncing around' of ideas which is so necessary for this type of creative work. Much of an architect's work concerns the accurate communication of design ideas to others involved in the project. Traditionally this involves the production of technical drawings, sketches and models by hand, although computer-generated images are playing an increasingly important role. Most architects, therefore, have as the focus of their workspace within an office a drawing board and/or CAD terminal where most of the creative work is done.

Other regularly visited parts of a busy architect's office will be the technical library, full of the latest editions of various technical manuals, official manuals such as the Building Regulations, manufacturers' literature and trade and professional journals; the print room where drawings which are normally done on transparent paper can be copied and sent out; and the meeting room where the latest developments on a particular job can be discussed with the relevant people.

What qualifications will I need?

Architect

To become an architect in the UK you must pass Parts 1 and 2 of the Royal Institute of British Architects (RIBA) Examination in Architecture and the RIBA Examination in Professional Practice (formerly RIBA Part 3). The majority of architects currently entering the profession in this country do so via one of the schools of architecture offering a course recognised by RIBA.

While entry requirements differ slightly between schools, you will normally need at least two academic subjects at A-level, or one A- and two AS-levels. (Applicants should note that in some schools Engineering Drawing A-level is not acceptable.) In addition, you must have passed at least five GCSEs including English Language, Maths and two science subjects. The RIBA recommends that at least three of the GCSE subjects are different to the A-level subjects. Some schools accept BTEC (or SCOTVEC) Certificates in Building Studies instead of A-levels, and work experience may be considered for mature students. A handful of schools of architecture insist on Maths or a science at A-level, but most are flexible. Generally, all schools are looking for a good mix of science and art subjects at both GCSE and A-level.

Training to become an architect takes a minimum of seven years. A three-year degree course (RIBA Part 1) is generally followed by a year working in an architects' office. Some students choose to spend their 'year out' working abroad, or in another area of the building industry. The next two years are spent back at architecture school

17

studying for the Diploma in Architecture (RIBA Part 2), although this does not have to be at the same school as the degree. The Diploma is followed by another year (minimum) working in an office before the Examination in Professional Practice can be taken (formerly RIBA Part 3). On passing this final examination candidates are eligible to become a full member of RIBA, and to register with the Architects' Registration Council of the UK (ARCUK).

If you are already working in an architects' office and are considering training as an architect, RIBA offers a part-time qualification route at a few schools. It is also possible to gain exemption from the degree (RIBA Part 1) and even the Diploma (RIBA Part 2) if you have sufficient certified practical experience. See page 24 for further details.

Architectural technologist (technician)

To become an architectural technologist you will generally be expected to work towards membership of the British Institute of Architectural Technologists (BIAT). The different classes of membership of BIAT are as follows: Member; Associate; Profile member; Student member; and Retired member. The requirements for each class of membership are given below. Which ever option you decide upon, useful subjects to study at GCSE include Maths, science subjects, Technology, Art and English.

Member (MBIAT)

There are three post-GCSE options for this category of membership: A/AS-levels in science and technology subjects; a BTEC National Certificate or Diploma in Building Studies; or a GNVQ in the Built Environment (Advanced level). In all cases these must be followed by either a degree in Architectural Technology or a related subject; or an HNC/HND in Building Studies with architectural options.

In addition, you will have to complete a two-year practice qualification logbook under the supervision of an approved supervisor. A further year of work experience is required for those who have followed a full-time course of study. Finally, you must pass a professional interview.

Associate (ABIAT)

Because of the increasingly complex and technically demanding nature of its members' work, BIAT has recently entered a transitional phase during which a first degree in Architectural Technology or a technologically based Built Environment degree will become the minimum educational qualification for entry as an Associate (ABIAT). In the meantime, however, BTEC/SCOTVEC HND/HNC courses will continue to be accepted. All courses must be approved by the Institute, who will be pleased to provide a full list on request.

Although entitled to use the professional designation ABIAT, Associate members may not practice on their own account. Associate members who wish to become self-employed should contact the Institute for guidance, where they will normally be re-registered as Profile members.

Profile member

Candidates who are not eligible for one of the standard routes of entry detailed above may become a Profile member and progress through one of three profiling routes:

- Route 1 is for applicants without full standard qualifications.
- Route 2 is for applicants with non-standard (including overseas) qualifications. You might be asked to submit your course documentation for assessment by the Institute.
- Route 3 is for applicants aged 30 years and over with at least ten years' relevant experience and with or without formal qualifications.

Student member

Any student at university, college or school, following a course designed to lead to a career in architectural technology is eligible for this category of BIAT membership.

Retired member

This is a special class of BIAT membership for those who have retired from full-time employment.

Note: the address for BIAT is given on page 59.

What personal skills and attitudes are needed?

Architect

All buildings are the product of compromise. The number of contributory factors which affect the design and production of even the smallest project have rendered this inevitable. As society becomes more complex and technology advances, so the compromise becomes greater.

One of the most important qualities a modern architect can possess is therefore the ability to juggle the requirements of the different professionals involved on the project through to a mutually satisfactory conclusion without any dilution of the original design concept. In short, an architect must be both visionary and diplomatic.

Other key skills for an architect are as follows:

Communication skills – the effective communication of ideas, knowledge and opinions is central to an architect's work. The ability to express ideas visually through sketches, drawings or models, as well as through the spoken and written word, is therefore essential.

Problem-solving – much of an architect's work concerns finding practical, elegant solutions to the various problems thrown up by the project. Architects tend to view problems as challenges or opportunities, aiming to solve them in as lateral and creative a way as possible. This approach can often make all the difference to the finished building.

Diplomacy – the requirements of other professionals working on a project, not to mention those of the client, can often seem completely at odds with what the architect wants to achieve and believes to be right. Sensitive handling of such situations is therefore an important skill.

Art/science balance – one of the continual struggles an architect faces is the tempering of a design concept by practicalities of structure and planning. A good architect therefore needs to be able to balance the practical and logical with the artistic and creative.

Sensitivity – architects create the spaces and places in which others live, work and play. Because what they do is so visible, it is important that architects are sensitive towards the environment, the public viewpoint, the clients' requirements, other professionals' requirements, so that their work offends as few people as possible.

Management skills – as head of the design team, the architect has to be a good manager both of his own staff and of other professionals. In addition, as you progress through your career as an architect, the amount of management and administration work you do is likely to outweigh the design work, and therefore good time management skills are also crucial.

Numeracy – a high level of numeracy is very important when working as an architect, and many schools still stipulate A-level Mathematics as an entry requirement. Everyday work such as producing scale drawings, surveying existing buildings and sites, and calculating the insulation properties of a composite wall all require basic numeracy. More complex mathematics are involved when designing the structure of the building (in short, whether or not it will stand up), and, although this is the structural engineer's job, the architect has to have a working knowledge of structure in order to discuss the building in the engineer's terms. On smaller buildings, where structural engineers are often not used, the architect will have to produce structural drawings and calculations.

Robustness and flexibility – when you have worked hard to come up with a good design which you know is right, it is not always easy to accept alterations. However, issues such as the clients' lack of money or vision; last-minute changes in the brief; planning, legal, fire or conservation regulations; and structural alterations, can all lead to major changes and sometimes even to the termination of a project. As with all creative subjects, architects can become protective about their work, but this should not be allowed to obstruct the right course of action.

Commitment – in many ways the seven years of architectural training acts as its own filter for the uncommitted. It is a long, tough course and in most schools the architects' studio lights burn through the night. This, however, is necessary preparation for work within the profession. Most architects' practices are small, and most small practices will require a certain number of late nights and weekends to be worked without paying overtime, in order to meet schedule deadlines.

Creativity – it sounds obvious, but if you are not a naturally creative person you probably will not make a good architect. Several schools list A-level Art as a preference, and all schools will want to see a portfolio of art work before places are awarded.

Left-handedness – this might sound odd, but surveys consistently show the proportion of architects who are left-handed to be over twice the national average. Medical science shows that left-handed people have a better perception of three-dimensional space, and this statistic is therefore hardly surprising. But right-handers need not worry; many of the world's leading architects are also right-handed.

Natural ability to make or mend things – much of what an architect does concerns understanding how things are put together, and how to convert two-dimensional drawings into three-dimensional objects. If you are interested in making things, mending things or simply dismantling things then you will already have acquired some of the skills needed to become a good architect.

Architectural technologist (technician)

It is the technician's job to turn the architect's concept into a reality, and a good technician will therefore act as a practical foil to the architect's creativity. While many of the skills and attributes listed above are also important for technicians, the following are also important:

Attention to detail – all drawings and models are done to scale (typically 1:100 or 1:200 for plans, sections and elevations), and a high degree of accuracy is necessary to ensure that everything fits when scaled up to life size on site.

Lateral thinking – the technician will often have to think laterally about the design itself, and in particular the consequences of any changes made. A simple example would be where the client looks at the plan and decides an extra window is needed to provide more natural light. The technician then has to see how the new window looks from the outside, assess the structural implications, check whether the new window affects the fire or planning regulations, and many other knock-on effects.

Problem-solving – when producing the detailed 'working drawings' for a building from the architect's design drawings, many problems will be thrown up. While working closely with the architect during this phase of the design, a good technician will have to be as inventive and creative as possible in solving these problems to avoid making unnecessary changes to the design itself.

How do I get into this work?

Below are the latest figures from UCAS for applicants to architecture courses at universities in the UK.

	Men	**Women**	**Total**
Applied	2336	901	3237
Accepted	1518	641	2159
Success-rate	(65%)	(71%)	(67%)

Following the recent rationalisation of training methods by RIBA, there are now three different ways you can train to become an architect: full-time study; part-time study; or by sitting the RIBA external exams. Each of these involves passing, or gaining exemption from, the following RIBA examinations:

- RIBA Examination in Architecture: Part 1
- RIBA Examination in Architecture: Part 2
- RIBA Examination in Professional Practice

In all cases, these examinations must be accompanied by a certified period of practical training of at least two years.

Architect: Full-time study

The majority of entrants to architectural training (94%) attend a full-time course at a school of architecture approved by RIBA. Of the 39 schools currently in the UK, 35 are in universities, two are affiliated to art colleges (the Kent Institute of Art and Design in Canterbury and the Royal College of Art in London) and two are independent (the Architectural Association and the Prince of Wales's Institute of Architecture, both in London). If you are currently at school and considering training as an architect, you will need to make some important post-GCSE decisions to enure that you have the right GCSEs and A-levels when you come to apply. Entry requirements for each school are different, so it's worth spending some time before you begin your A-level courses finding out which school(s) you would like to go to, and what their specific requirements are.

Architect: Part-time study

If you are currently working in an architects' office, you can train to become an architect on a part-time day-release basis. Requirements for part-time students are identical to those for full-time students, and the amount of time needed to study while carrying out a full-time job should not be underestimated. Part-time students typically spend four years gaining RIBA Part 1 (instead of the usual three) and three years instead of two gaining RIBA Part 2. In 1995, 5% of entrants to architectural training were part-time students.

Architect: External candidates

There is a small group of students each year (1% in 1995) for whom full- or part-time study is not appropriate or possible, but who, nevertheless, are eligible to take up architectural training. This group includes:

- students with extensive practical experience
- students who have already studied architecture – either in the UK or overseas – but who ended their studies without passing the exams
- students with professional or academic qualifications related to architecture.

For these students, RIBA has devised a special route to qualification heavily weighted towards relevant practical experience, and with fewer examinations and projects. RIBA puts an upper limit on the number of students taking this route each year, as each applicant has to be assessed individually to determine the level of experience gained.

Architectural technologist (technician)

For those who have chosen to make architectural technology their career, qualifying as a full member of BIAT is an essential stepping stone. An increasing number of architectural practices and other employers are insisting that the architectural technologists on their staff have qualified through the Institute.

BIAT operates a network of 15 regional centres within the UK through which student members can get involved with the professional community, establish contacts, gain an insight into the opportunities open to them, and learn from the technical expertise of qualified members.

What should I do now to prepare?

General

In the period leading up to your application to architecture school, try to find out as much as you can about the profession and about buildings themselves. Visit your school careers library to research the various courses and options. Read the daily newspapers (many have an architecture section) and have a look at the main trade journals (see page 57).

Perhaps most importantly of all, try to develop an awareness of the buildings you are in and around from day to day. When do you think your house or school were built? What are the obvious means of support for ceilings, window openings and staircases? How might the building have been assembled and what is it made of? How much extra would the roof weigh if it was covered in snow? You don't actually have to know or even find out the answers to any of these questions – but you should get into the habit of asking them.

You might also consider visiting the local town hall and looking at some pending planning applications. Try also to take notice of the buildings you walk past, through, underneath or over. And remember that building sites will become your second home, so don't just walk past them like everyone else does, but have a good look – you will learn a lot about basic construction techniques if you do.

GCSEs and A-levels

Although entry requirements differ from school to school, there are some common factors. You should ensure as far as possible that you have a good mixture of arts and science subjects at GCSE. You

27

might be able to even out an arts or science bias by taking another GCSE while you are doing your A-levels.

A good art/science combination is also desirable at A-level, although this is not always possible due to timetable restrictions. Check individual architecture school requirements as some will ask for Maths A-level. Art at GCSE and/or A-level will also be very useful.

Portfolio

The ability to communicate ideas through drawings and sketches is central to an architect's work, and most schools of architecture will ask you to show a portfolio of work demonstrating your ability in this area. Do not underestimate the amount of time it will take to prepare your portfolio. GCSE and A-level art students will be able to include much of their coursework, but remember you are applying for a course in architecture and it is therefore advisable that your portfolio contains some drawings, sketches, models or photographs of buildings. Technical drawing skills are not necessary at this stage as these will be learnt at architecture school.

Work experience

While work experience before the beginning of an architectural course is not a requirement, it would undoubtedly be useful in helping you decide whether you enjoy and are suited to the work, and would go down well with admissions tutors. No amount of reading or study can replace hands-on experience and contact with professionals actually doing the job. If work experience is not possible, a short interview with a practising architect would give you some useful insights, and might also prove useful when looking for a 'year out' placement after your degree.

Work experience need not necessarily be in an architects' office. For example, you will learn a tremendous amount by labouring on a building site, or perhaps assisting your parents or a friend or colleague with any building work they might be doing – even if it's only erecting a garden shed or greenhouse.

If no work experience is available, you could try simply measuring a building (eg your house) and then drawing plans and elevations to scale. This kind of initiative could make all the difference on the UCAS form or in an interview.

What are the good and bad aspects of the work?

Pros

The most rewarding aspect of an architect's work must be the sheer job satisfaction: few careers can offer the sense of achievement which comes from seeing your designs, concepts and ideas converted into full-scale buildings in which people live, work and enjoy themselves. Another plus is the variety of opportunity within the profession – jobs with large or small companies, in any number of specialist areas, in almost any country in the world.

Many young architects find that a high level of responsibility comes quite quickly after qualification – running a sizable project during the first year of employment is not uncommon, and many architects feel able to set up their own business comparatively early in their career.

The skills gained as an architect will enable you to do what you want with your own house – alterations, extensions or even a brand new building.

Cons

The building industry is very sensitive to changes in the economy, and is always hit hard by recession. Because of the cyclical nature of macro-economics, and the length of the course, it is possible for student architects to begin their training during a time of great buoyancy within the building industry, and to qualify seven years later during a bad recession with very little hope of getting a job.

Architects are very much beholden to their clients and to the various regulatory authorities. Design concepts, however good, are nearly always watered down and every finished building is a compromise.

On large projects within large practices it is possible for newly qualified architects to get stuck on the details of the building and to lose track of the overall concept of the project, and of the developments within the profession itself. You will also invariably find that as you progress within the profession, the ratio of design to management changes in favour of management.

It has been stated that architects are generally paid less than many of their professional counterparts. This is accompanied by the public perception of the value of the service an architect provides being much lower than, for example, a doctor or lawyer.

Finally, because buildings are such a familiar part of everyday life, the skills of an architect tend to be undervalued compared with those of, say, a solicitor or accountant, and you will therefore find that your friends will always want you to work for next to nothing!

Who will I work with?

During your career as an architect you will probably work with people from most of the other building industry disciplines including civil and structural engineers, building services engineers, construction and building management professionals, quantity surveyors, surveyors and town planners. There is also a wide range of careers within the architectural profession itself: architects, project architects, technicians, secretarial support staff, interior designers, landscape architects, computer–aided design (CAD) technicians, model-makers, perspective artists, photographers – as well as an almost infinite number of specialist careers such as construction lawyers, architectural journalists, lecturers, lighting or acoustics engineers and architectural historians.

The client

The client is the person or body who commissions the building. This can range from an individual commissioning a private house or extension to an organisation such as a company, local authority or charity. It is normally only the senior architects within a practice who deal with the client, although the level of involvement a client has with the design team during the design of the building will vary.

The design team

The design team has already been mentioned several times. This is the team of architects, technicians and specialists (such as structural engineer, services engineers and quantity surveyor) who produce the building design under the direction of the project architect. Working as an architect you will spend much of your time as part of, or in charge of, a design team.

Builders

Once the detailed design or 'working' drawings have been completed, they are sent to the quantity surveyor who measures the amount of each material required, as well as services, equipment and labour, and produces an extensive document known as the Bill of Quantities. This is then sent, along with a complete set of drawings, to a number of builders who submit tenders, or prices, for the work.

Once a builder is chosen, the client appoints a clerk of works who, together with the architect, liaise closely with the builder on site, via regular site meetings, to ensure that the work is being carried out to a satisfactory standard, and in accordance with the drawings.

The architect will spend much of his time on site during the construction stages of a building. During this time it is important to try and develop a working knowledge of the large number of skilled crafts involved in producing a new building. Architects should be able to converse with bricklayers, carpenters, electricians, plasterers, etc using the correct terminology involved with these different skills.

Regulatory authorities

At roughly the same time as the builders are invited to tender, a set of drawings is also sent to the various regulatory authorities for their approval. The authorities consulted will depend upon the type, proposed usage and location of the building – for example, English Heritage might need to be consulted for work on or next to an important historic building or site. All building work, however, must be given both Building Regulations approval and planning permission by the local council. In addition, once Building Regulations approval has been granted, a Building Inspector from the local authority will make inspections on site at various stages during the buildings' construction to ensure that the work is being carried out satisfactorily. It is also necessary for most projects to consult with specially trained fire officers either at the local fire station, or at fire service headquarters.

What will I earn?

Compared with most other professions, architecture is not particularly well paid. The 1994 median annual salary for architects working in the UK was £22,956, and for architects aged under 30 it was £15,900. Even for principals of private practices the figure was only £25,000, although it should be borne in mind that most private practices are very small. For principal partners in large practices it was around £41,000, and in most cases this would come with benefits such as a car, pension, private health care and a bonus.

There is also variation from region to region and from practice to practice. London pays more than the rest of the country, large firms generally pay more than small ones, with commercial and industrial firms paying the most.

It is important to note, however, that for a young architect the quality and variety of work undertaken during the first few years are every bit as important as the salary, and in many cases some of the less well-paid jobs will provide a much broader experience and higher level of responsibility than those with the more attractive salaries.

What are the hours and holidays like?

It is in the nature of architecture, as with many design-related disciplines, that the designer is never quite satisfied with what he/she has done, and therefore corrections and improvements are often made right up until the last minute. Consequently architects are required to work long hours, perhaps finishing drawings for a presentation to a client or getting a competition entry ready to meet the deadline. The frequency of such long hours will depend very much on the specific workload and scheduling of the firm concerned, but the ethic of working late will by this time have long been ingrained into your way of life from your college days where staying up late (and sometimes all night) in the design studio to finish projects is the norm rather than the exception.

For architects working in the UK, the average holiday entitlement in 1994 was 23 days per annum, which corresponds with the normal entitlement of 20 days for a new job, increasing after a certain number of years (usually five) by one day a year.

Will I meet the public?

Generally speaking, no. Architects are employed by a client to produce a building which they do in consultation with various other professionals. Most of the work is done either in the office or on site. However, during those parts of the work which are carried out outside, such as site visits and surveys, architects will inevitably have a small amount of contact with the public.

There might also be occasions where the architect is required to speak at a town, city or county council meeting in order to argue the case for a new building on behalf of his or her client. This would usually only occur where an objection had been made, and such situations can often lead to confrontation with the public.

In addition, there could be certain special occasions where an architect might meet the public: a particular building or development might win an award for which there would be a presentation ceremony; alternatively, a prestigious building might be officially opened by a celebrity or dignitary.

Finally, if you become famous or notorious, even at a local level, you might well be asked to make various after-dinner speeches, and give seminars and lectures.

What insights will this work give me?

Each project you work on will bring with it a new set of challenges. As you work on the project you will be addressing these challenges, overcoming problems, and gaining new insights. Here are just a few examples:

- Building types – Any building project you work on will bring new insights and knowledge specific to that area of business, industry or work, eg prison, auditorium, sports centre, school, airport.

- Building construction – The way that buildings are put together is both fascinating and a mystery to most people. Whether on new or old buildings, your work as an architect will bring an understanding of construction which will underpin your whole career.

- Local knowledge – You will inevitably become very knowledgeable about each of the different sites you work on. Information on the surrounding topography, local features, cultural aspects, etc are all important. Some of this knowledge will be part of your research, some will be picked up, but all of it will give you an insight to that particular area.

- Government plans – Part of your research for any site will involve looking at the local government Structure Plan for that county or area. These plans earmark specific areas for certain types of development, eg domestic, retail or business, and are produced to ensure that the development of the country as a whole is along lines agreed by the government. Structure Plans also define green belt areas and National Parks, ensuring that they remain protected.

- National/international events – As an architect you will be working in an industry which is frequently at the centre of major events and celebrations, eg the millennium celebrations or the Olympic Games. Your interest in and knowledge of these things will be heightened by reading professional journals, and possibly even becoming involved in the design of such projects.

- Social awareness – A lot can be discovered about the social climate within a particular area by looking at the surrounding buildings, public spaces and general 'urban fabric'. Whether you are designing a project within an area, or are simply a curious visitor, your architectural training will heighten your awareness of the prevailing social and economic climate.

- History – It is true of many disciplines that there are often some good lessons to be learned by looking at history. This is certainly true of architecture. One of the most fascinating aspects of training to be an architect is learning about the great buildings, builders and architects throughout the world who have gone before. A knowledge of architectural history brings with it insights into international social history and culture – and encourages you to take notice of, and learn from, your surroundings.

Are the prospects good for my career?

Generally speaking, yes. After a long and demanding qualification period you will be eligible to register with the Architects' Registration Council of the UK (ARCUK), join one of the professional architectural institutions such as the Royal Institute of British Architects (RIBA) and enter a well-established industry, for which there will always be a demand. Moving between jobs and entering new areas of specialisation are comparatively easy to do, and since the majority of architectural practices is small (63% have fewer than ten staff) many architects are able to set up on their own soon after joining the profession – often within as little as five years after qualification. In addition, UK architectural qualifications are accepted around the world, so a move to another country, if desired, should be comparatively easy from a professional viewpoint.

However, the effects of changes in the national economy on the building industry can be dramatic, and with a seven-year training period it would be possible to begin your qualification during a boom, and to qualify during a recession and find that there is no work.

Architecture and the building industry itself are also constantly developing to reflect changes in the social, political and technological environment which surrounds them. As with any profession, such developments will generate the need for new areas of expertise, as well as spell the end for some of the older ones. Architects must therefore remain sensitive to changes occurring within the broader profession and ensure that they equip themselves with appropriate skills to keep up.

39

What about training at work?

As has been mentioned before, a minimum of two years' practical experience working in an office is required in order to qualify as an architect or as an architectural technologist. It should also be stressed that with architecture, possibly more than any other profession, the real learning process does not begin until you are in your first job producing live working drawings, sorting out problems on site and dealing day to day with the other professionals in the field. It can come as a shock having done seven years training to discover, when you begin your first job, that an eighteen-year-old apprentice technician knows far more about the practical aspects of building than a newly qualified architect.

Architect

If you are currently working in an architect's office, you can train to become an architect on a part-time basis. Requirements for part-time students are identical to those for full-time students, and the amount of time needed to study while carrying out a full-time job should not be underestimated. Part-time students typically spend four years gaining RIBA Part 1 (instead of the usual three) and three years instead of two gaining RIBA Part 2.

RIBA has also recently devised a special route to qualification for students with extensive practical experience, but with no formal architectural qualifications, which puts emphasis on practical knowledge, with fewer examinations and projects. RIBA puts an upper limit on the number of students taking this route each year, as each applicant has to be assessed individually to determine the level of experience gained.

Architectural technologist

A special BIAT qualification route exists (Route 3) specifically for applicants aged 30 years and over with at least ten years' relevant experience and with or without formal qualifications.

What are the recent developments in this area?

Architecture and the building industry itself are constantly developing to reflect changes in the social, political and technological environment which surrounds them. Here are a few of the recent developments.

Information technology

Developments in IT have transformed the way in which the modern architect works. Most notably, the introduction of computer-aided design (CAD) software has in many cases all but eradicated the traditional drawing board and pens. Drawings can be produced and modified on screen, and need not be printed until they are finalised.

Sophisticated three-dimensional modelling software has been developed which enables the client to be given a guided 'video' tour of the building and its site including trees, cars, people, surrounding buildings and natural and artificial lighting effects before any building work has been carried out.

In addition, the advent of e-mail and the Internet means that we cannot be very far away from the 'virtual drawing' – electronic images transmitted from the architects' office to the site and used and built from without a sheet of paper anywhere. The drawings would then be stored electronically rather than in the cumbersome A0-sized chests which are currently still to be found in most practices.

Materials

Architects are continually being bombarded with salesmen demonstrating the latest roof tiles, insulation, cladding, etc – so much so that it is impossible to keep abreast of every new product. Developments in materials science and knowledge are reflected in the range and types of building products available. Advances in polymer science in particular have given today's architects a range of materials which were not available ten years ago such as 'intumescent' paint (used to paint exposed structural steelwork) which expands into a heat-resistant foam during a fire.

Energy

Dwindling supplies of fossil fuels have led to a heightened awareness of the importance of conserving energy. The UK Building Regulations now specify minimum insulation levels for all external building elements (including floors), and in some Scandinavian countries the development of technologies such as argon-filled triple-glazing and super insulation have led to the creation of houses in which the occupiers hardly ever need to switch on the heating.

Environment

Awareness of the importance of the natural environment is currently at an all-time high. It is therefore very important that today's architects are sensitive in their designs and think carefully about the use of materials, natural light, methods of waste disposal and landscaping.

Will I need other languages for the work?

You will not need to speak another language in order to progress and be successful as an architect in the UK. However, as Britain becomes increasingly involved with other European countries, many architectural practices will be seeking work abroad, in the same way that many European architects will be looking to expand their business into the UK. Specific areas which need to be addressed in these cases include:

- learning the differences in building regulations and planning restrictions of another country

- becoming acquainted with foreign building culture and history

- developing a working knowledge of the infrastructure and standard working practices of an unfamiliar building industry.

Obviously in this situation fluency in, or even a working knowledge of, a language other than English would be a clear advantage, even though much international European business is conducted in English.

Practices with a particular area of expertise might become involved in work in any number of non-English speaking countries. For instance, a company specialising in the design of concert halls and auditoria might find that only a handful of such buildings are commissioned each year throughout the world. A second language when working for a company with this level of specialisation could therefore lead to a high level of involvement in some very exciting projects in countries where that language was spoken.

Will I be able to work overseas or travel for my job?

Overseas travel

Your first chance to travel overseas once en route to becoming an architect will almost certainly come at university or college. Most architecture schools include, as part of the training, at least one foreign trip (and sometimes more) to allow students the chance to experience and study the architecture and building culture of other countries. Details of any overseas trips to be undertaken as part of the training will be given in the individual institution prospectuses.

Once you are working as an architect, overseas travel is certainly possible. A position in one of the larger and more prestigious architectural firms could bring with it opportunities to travel and work almost anywhere in the world. Similarly, as Britain moves closer to becoming a part of Europe, an increasing number of smaller practices are also looking for work overseas – in the same way that European firms are looking to the UK to expand their business.

However, overseas travel cannot be guaranteed. Many practices will have enough work within the UK, and foreign travel might not therefore be necessary for any of its employees.

Whether or not you get the chance to travel with your job, an architectural training usually fosters within its students a passion for the subject, and many architects travel extensively in order to see the world's greatest architectural accomplishments.

Domestic travel

While overseas travel cannot be guaranteed, travel within the UK is more often than not an intrinsic part of any architect's work. It would be usual for even the smallest firms to be running simultaneous jobs in a number of different areas, and since no architectural project can be managed entirely from the office, architects often have to travel over a wide area in order to attend regular site visits.

Will I use computers in this work?

The technological advances which have been made within the IT industry over the past two decades have had a dramatic impact on the architectural profession. Software for simply producing drawings on screen rather than by hand on tracing paper has meant that messy corrections which used to involve scraping ink off the surface of the tracing paper with a razor blade can now be done at the press of a button. Repeating elements such as windows, doors and indeed whole floors for multi-level buildings now need only be drawn once rather than copied over and over again by hand. Multiple drawing layers mean that the structural plans, heating and ventilation plans, electrical plan, landscaping plan and materials plan (and many more) can all be overlaid on to a single floor plan drawing rather than painstakingly copied out. When the drawing is finished, it is literally 'drawn' by a high–speed mechanical plotter which actually creates the image by using pens on paper.

Sophisticated three-dimensional modelling software has also been developed which enables the architect to create three-dimensional colour views of the building on-screen. The effects of natural and artificial lighting can be reproduced and assessed, and on the best systems the client can be given a guided 'video' tour of the building inside and out, and the site, before any work has been carried out.

Most schools of architecture now have fairly sophisticated Computer- aided design (CAD) systems, and much of the coursework is now being done on computer rather than at the drawing board.

47

Could I become famous?

It is more likely that one of your buildings will achieve either fame or notoriety than that you yourself will become a household name. Thus the Canary Wharf Tower, the National Gallery Extension, the Sydney Opera House and the Houses of Parliament are all more famous than their respective architects IM. Pei, Robert Venturi, Jorn Utson and Sir Charles Barry. (One notable exception might be St Paul's Cathedral whose architect Sir Christopher Wren is as famous as his buildings!)

However, a general increase in awareness of architecture and the built environment, famously championed by Prince Charles, has led to the emergence of a number of modern-day architecture personalities and political figures, chief among them:

- (Lord) Richard Rogers (Lloyd's Building in London and the Pompidou Centre in Paris, with Renzo Piano), famous for putting all the innards of his buildings on the outside, and for his plans for central London which include the pedestrianisation of Trafalgar Square and the Embankment

- Sir Norman Foster (Hong Kong and Shanghai Bank in Hong Kong, and Stansted Airport, Stansted), famous for being the pioneer of high-tech architecture

The chances of becoming this well-known on the international architecture scene are extremely slim. But each of these architects, and other famous names both here and abroad, run large practices, often with offices in various countries, and if you are good enough, and more specifically if your designs are in the right style, you might well be able to get a job with one of the stars.

Could I work independently?

At one level, yes. Most architectural practices employ fewer than ten people, and 30% of those in the UK employ only one or two architects. Obviously many architects are setting up on their own, or with a partner, and are being successful. However, doing this will inevitably bring restrictions to the type and size of projects which you are able to handle. Most one- or two-man band practices will be carrying out work up to a maximum project value of around £500,000. This would include, for example, one-off houses, small schools and libraries, etc and all kinds of renovation work. Airports, hospitals, large office or shopping complexes, auditoria and stadiums would all be far too large to handle.

Possibly the greatest independence is to be gained by working as a self-employed architect, technician or surveyor on a freelance basis. By contracting your services out to other companies you will have total control over the amount and type of work you do, though of course you will always have to work to your client's budget and deadlines.

However, at another level, it is not possible for an architect to work independently. An architect's work necessarily involves interaction with a large number of outside professionals and services, without whom no building project would ever get off the ground. This, therefore, is definitely not the profession for a reclusive type who does not like getting out and meeting people.

What other considerations are there?

A number of additional issues – some important and others merely interesting – fall outside the scope of the questions which have been asked so far. In no particular order, these are listed below.

Women on site

Mention should be made of the fact that, like it or not, the building industry (although, not necessarily the architectural profession itself) is a male-dominated business. Many of the associated professions such as structural engineering, services engineering and building are predominantly male. Building sites in particular are places where you will find mostly men working, and, depending upon the personality of the individual, some women architects might find such an environment uncomfortable.

Cost of materials at college

Dependent upon the particular course or options you take when going to architecture school, student architects are often required to equip themselves throughout the course, and during the first term in particular, with high-quality and often therefore expensive drawing equipment and materials. Even if you opt for a course where most of the design work is done on a computer, you will have to print your final drawings on to paper (often A1-sized) and then 'render' them for your presentation.

The 'crit'

During the course of their professional lives, architects are often required to communicate their designs, concepts and ideas to individuals and groups of people through formal presentations involving drawings, models, photographs and sometimes computer simulations and other media. Many people do not find this type of presentation easy, and it is for this reason that the architectural training encourages its students from the outset to present their work to the other students and tutors on the course via informal 'critique' sessions.

These 'crits', as they are often called, are an excellent way of learning, and offer the best opportunity to see the work your student colleagues are producing. However, for many students these presentations can be a nerve-racking ordeal, and anyone thinking of going to architecture school should aim to become competent in this style of open presentation.

Architecture as an art

It might not be immediately apparent to those studying architecture that this discipline is regarded by the artistic community, and historically, as one of the arts. Throughout history the various artistic styles prevalent during a particular period are mirrored by a style in architecture bearing the same name and the same artistic traits. Thus we have labels such as Classical, Baroque, Gothic, Renaissance, Arts and Crafts, Art Nouveau, Modern and Post-modern for the different architectural styles which were fashionable during those periods of history/art. It is important for architects to be aware of the changing fashions of the day, and also to be aware of the historic context in which they are practising their art.

How can I find out about the work?

Exhibitions/museums

A good way for prospective architects to learn more about the profession is to attend one of the wide variety of architectural exhibitions, degree shows or museums around the UK. Exhibitions are frequently mounted (especially in London) in order to give leading contemporary architects from all over the world the chance to display drawings, models and photographs of their latest projects. A number of permanent exhibitions and museums also exist, frequently within famous buildings themselves, such as the Lloyd's Building exhibition (4th floor, Lloyd's Building, London). Among the other architectural museums worth visiting are the Sir John Soane Museum in Lincoln's Inn Fields, London, and the Weald and Downland Museum in West Sussex.

You should also be aware that university and college architecture departments generally mount degree and diploma shows during June/July where members of the public are invited to view the work of the student architects. This is an excellent way for anyone considering entering architecture school to see the type and standard of the work they will be expected to produce.

Internet

There is a large amount of information relating to architecture on the Internet. All the architecture schools have sites which are worth looking at and some of the larger practices in the UK also have sites where you can look at the work they have done.

Books, journals and newspapers

The range of published material covering all aspects of architecture is so vast that it is often difficult for a prospective student architect to know what to read. Try choosing a book on a specific architect whose name you know, or whose work you like the look of from the cover. A quick look through some indexes might show that there are buildings by some well-known architects in your area which you could go and have a look at.

Among the various journals which are published, the most popular are the *Architects' Journal* (weekly) and the *Architectural Review* (monthly). These are read by most student and practising architects in the UK and elsewhere and are a good way of keeping up to date with the latest projects and news. You will also find that most quality newspapers have an architecture section or feature which offers a cheaper way of keeping abreast of the industry.

Television programmes

During recent years there has been a number of excellent television series and one-off documentaries covering the work of different architects (contemporary and historic) or addressing a range of architectural issues. Many of these will be available on video from the architecture library once you get to university or college. All the benefits normally associated with television make this an excellent medium by which to learn about large-scale and frequently one-off items such as buildings. With architecture as one of the key international issues leading up to the new millennium, there are sure to be some excellent television programmes covering the various world-wide projects.

Which courses and qualifications are available?

You may well by now have decided that you want to work/study in the construction industry but are still not sure which discipline to pursue. The range of post-16 courses and qualifications available for those wishing to enter the construction industry is enormous. It is therefore important that anyone wishing to enter one of the construction disciplines sets some time aside to research the types of course available – even if you think you know exactly what you want to do.

For those who ultimately choose work/study within the architectural profession, either as an architect or architectural technologist, the main types of course/qualification are given below. For those who are not sure, lists

of other related courses are also given.

Alternatives to A-levels
BTEC National Certificate/Diploma/HNC
Building Studies
Built Environment
Construction
Land Use

GNVQ (Advanced)
Built Environment
Construction

Architect
Degrees
Architecture (also called Architectural Design or Architectural Studies)

Postgraduate
Diploma in Architecture

Professional
For details of the professional

qualifications required to become an architect see page 24.

Architectural technologist
HNDs
Architectural Technology
Building Studies (Architectural Technology)

Professional
For details of the professional qualifications required to become an architectural technologist see page 00.

Others to consider
HNDs
Building
Building Services Engineering
Civil Engineering
Computer-Aided Engineering
Construction
Engineering
Estate Management
Estate Surveying
Interior Design
Land Administration
Land Surveying
Model-making
Quantity Surveying
Spatial Design
Surveying (Engineering)

Degrees
Building
Building Services Engineering
Building Surveying
Civil Engineering
Estate Management
Interior Design
Land Surveying
Landscape Architecture
Quantity Surveying
Town and Country Planning

Postgraduate
The two year Dip(Arch) qualification (RIBA part 2) which forms part of the normal architectural training is, of course, a postgraduate qualification. In addition, most UK schools of architecture do offer MA/MSc qualifications which can usually be taken either concurrently with the Dip(Arch) or afterwards. Such qualifications do not form part of the professional qualification programme, but can be useful – especially for students wishing to remain within the academic sector as a lecturer of architecture. PhD qualifications in architecture are also offered by some schools.

MA/MSc and PhD courses in architecture vary considerably, and it is therefore advisable to contact the individual schools for further information.

Which organisations should I contact?

Whichever construction industry discipline or profession you are considering, one of the best places to start looking for information is the relevant professional body. Prospective architects should contact the Royal Institute of British Architects (RIBA), either at the central office or at one of the regional branches, and those looking for a career in architectural technology should contact the British Institute of Architectural Technologists (BIAT).

High quality careers information relating to the industry as a whole, with special emphasis on working for construction companies, can be obtained from the Construction Industry Training Board (CITB).

For professional advice on the most appropriate course or career, contact your local careers service company, who will be able to help you decide which career is best for you, pinpoint your specific needs and point you in the right direction for further information.

Finally, the best way to find out more about a specific course is to contact the department running the course directly. You might be able to find out what you want over the phone or in a letter. Alternatively, all architecture schools have open days or exhibition times where you will be able to go and look round.

A list of useful addresses is given on page 59.

What publications should I look at?

Periodicals

Architects Journal (weekly)
Architectural Review (monthly)
Building Design (weekly)
RIBA Journal (monthly)

Books

Working In Construction, published by COIC
Working In Buildings and Property, published by COIC
Careers In Architecture, published by Kogan Page Limited
Careers and Courses in the Construction Industry, published by
the Construction Industry Training Board (CITB)
Art & Design Courses 1997–98, published by Trotman & Co. Ltd
Degree Course Offers, published by Trotman & Co. Ltd
Modern Architecture since 1900, by William J. R. Curtis, published
by Phaidon Press Limited
Architecture For Beginners, by Louis Hellman, published by Writers
and Readers Publishing Cooperative (Unwin)
Architecture: Form, Space and Order by Francis D.K. Ching,
published by Van Nostrand Reinhold Company, Inc.
A History Of Architecture, Sir Banister Fletcher, published by Athlone
Press

Leaflets

A Career In Architecture
Available from any branch of the Royal Institute of British Architects
(RIBA)

Qualify for a Professional Career as an Architectural Technologist
Education and Training for a Career in Architectural Technology
Becoming a Member
Directory of Approved Courses and CAD Directory
All available from the British Institute of Architectural Technologists
(BIAT)

Which addresses will help me?

Architects and Surveyors Institute (ASI)
St Mary House, 15 St Mary St,
Chippenham, Wiltshire SN15 3WD
Tel: 01249 444505/655398

Architects' Registration Council of the United Kingdom (ARCUK)
73 Hallam Street, London W1N 5LQ
Tel: 0171 580 5861

British Institute of Architectural Technologists (BIAT)
397 City Road, London EC1V 1NE
Tel: 0171 278 2206

Construction Industry Training Board (CITB)
Head Office
Bircham Newton, King's Lynn
Norfolk PE31 6RH
Tel: 01553 776677
Fax: 01553 691676

CITB Regional Offices
2 Kew Court, Pynes Hill
Rydon Lane, Exeter EX 5AZ
Tel: 01392 444900
Fax: 01392445044

Peverel House
The Green, Hatfield Peverel
Chelmsford, Essex CM3 2JG
Tel: 01245 380055
Fax: 01245 382444

Shenstone House, Dudley Rd
Halesowen, W Mids B63 3NT
Tel: 0121 585 5252
Fax: 0121 585 6092

8 Trafford Court, Trafford Way,
Doncaster DN1 1PN
Tel: 01302 323533
Fax: 01302 738305

Royal Institute of British Architects (RIBA)
66 Portland Place,
London W1N 4AD
Tel: 0171 580 5533

RIBA Eastern Region
6 King's Parade,
Cambridge CB2 1SJ
Tel: 01223 324157

RIBA East Midlands Region
3 St James's Terrace,
Nottingham NG1 6FW.
Tel: 0115 941 3650

RIBA London Region
66 Portland Place,
London W1N 4AD
Tel: 0171 580 5533

RIBA Northern Region
6 Higham Place, Newcastle
upon Tyne NE1 8AF
Tel: 0191 232 4436

RIBA North West Region
44–46 King Street, Knutsford,
Cheshire WA16 6HJ
Tel: 01565 652927

RIBA Southern Region
Massey's Folley, Church Road,
Upper Farringdon, Alton,
Hampshire GU34 3EG
Tel: 01420 587393

RIBA South East Region
15–17 Upper Grosvenor Road,
Tunbridge Wells, Kent TN1 2DU
Tel: 01892 515878

RIBA South Western Region
School of Architecture,
University of Plymouth, Notte
Street, Plymouth PL1 2AR
Tel: 01752 265921

RIBA Wessex Region
School of Architecture, University
of Bath, Bath BA2 7AY
Tel: 01225 826654

RIBA West Midlands Region
Birmingham and Midlands
Institute, Margaret Street,
Birmingham B1 3SP
Tel: 0121 233 2321

RIBA Yorkshire Region
8 Woodhouse Square,
Leeds LS3 1AD
Tel: 0113 245 6250

RIBA Wales Region
Society of Architects in Wales,
75a Llandennis Road,
Rhydypennau, Cardiff CF2 6EE
Tel: 01222 762215

**Royal Society of Ulster
Architects**
2 Mount Charles,
Belfast BT7 1NZ
Tel: 01232 323760

**Royal Incorporation of
Architects in Scotland**
15 Rutland Square,
Edinburgh EH1 2BE
Tel: 0131 229 7545/7205